NEWCASTLE UPON TYNE

Edited by Lynsey Hawkins

First published in Great Britain in 2003 by
YOUNG WRITERS
Remus House,
Coltsfoot Drive,
Peterborough, PE2 9JX
Telephone (01733) 890066

SB ISBN 1 84460 215 X

FOREWORD

Young Writers was established in 1991 as a foundation for promoting the reading and writing of poetry amongst children and young adults. Today it continues this quest and proceeds to nurture and guide the writing talents of today's youth.

From this year's competition Young Writers is proud to present a showcase of the best poetic talent from across the UK. Each hand-picked poem has been carefully chosen from over 66,000 'Hullabaloo!' entries to be published in this, our eleventh primary school series.

This year in particular we have been wholeheartedly impressed with the quality of entries received. The thought, effort, imagination and hard work put into each poem impressed us all and once again the task of editing was a difficult but enjoyable experience.

We hope you are as pleased as we are with the final selection and that you and your family will continue to be entertained with *Hullabaloo! Newcastle Upon Tyne* for many years to come.

CONTENTS

La Sagesse Junior School

Charlotte Gilroy	28
Emma Donohoe	29
Lisa Chambers	30
Charlotte Hudson	31
Eleanor Reynolds	32
Megan Roberts	33
Amelia Armstrong	34
Sarah Gourley	35
Caroline Dixon	36
Ciara McFaul	37
Scarlett Coles	38
Jessica Fulgenzi	39
Lara Allen	40
Francesca Ayre	41
Katie Crumbley	42
Lucy O'Donnell	43
Beth Watson	44
Claire Allen	45
Philippa Mulgrove	46
Jessica Bell	47
Charlotte Bennetts	48

St Mark's RC Primary School, Westerhope

Lee Summers	49
Laura Simpson	50
James Roberts	51
Ross Minto	52
Sam Monkhouse	53
Stephanie Corbett	54
Liam Collins	55
Lucy Potts	56
Autumn Irving-Carr	57
Sophie Monaghan	58
Callum Rankin	59
Debra Webb	60

Jake Sturrock	94
Kathryn Rutherford	95
Megan Peterson	96
Iain Nicholson	97
Christopher Neve	98
Matthew Neve	99
Emily Miller	100
Sophie Loughlen	101
Adam Lewis	102
Jessica Hindson	103
Ellen Hayes	104
Ruby Friel	105
Bethany Foster	106
Rachel Farrey	107
Joshua Crabtree	108
Oliver Cooke	109
Abby Cairns	110
Alexander Brissenden-Ruddy	111
Elleanor Boyle	112
Thomas Bewick	113
Liam Anderson	114
Brooke Cairns	115
Sophie Dorner	116
Adam Berkeley	117
David Goldsmith	118
Alex Robinson	119
Jairaj Lalli	120
Laura Convery	121
Joel Nickerson	122
Rachel Hirst	123
Stephanie Gentles	124
Jordan Gray	125
Amy Bolam	126
Jennifer Spencer	127
Brooke Black	128
Steffie Loughlen	130

The Poems

IN MY PLANET 'MILKY WAY'

In my planet *'Milky Way'*
Everything is out of the way,
All the petals are made out of silk,
And the rivers flow full of milk.
The plants and trees all talk,
And in the mornings, they have a jolly good walk.

There is lots of food everywhere,
And there is no time to stand and stare.
There are ladders made out of leather,
And there are chairs made out of feather.
The houses are made out of gingerbread,
And the boxes are made out of pencil lead.
In my planet *'Milky Way'*.

Mangoes jog, oranges run,
Bananas and apples dance everywhere.
Chocolates and toffees talk on the phone,
Animals walk without any bone.
In my planet *'Milky Way'*.

Arushi Sharma (11)
Cragside Primary School

THE BLACK AND WHITE DOG

I take my dog
into the fog
around the park and back
he is black and white and also fab
he has blue eyes
and sensitive ears.
Malcolm is his name
his ball I aim
sometimes in the bin.
At home he runs all about
so we have to shout.
When he's been fed
he goes to bed.
When he's awake
we take him around the lake.

Shaunie Branighan (11)
Cragside Primary School

KING HENRY

King Henry was tall and fat and bold
Had his own armour and owned tons of gold
Six wives, six wives, six wives he had
Were executed, divorced and died, for Henry was mad.

Christopher Mole (10)
Cragside Primary School

FUSS TO HULLABALOO

Fuss is disturbance,
Disturbance is commotion,
Commotion is hubbub,
Hubbub is noise,
Noise is din,
Din is uproar,
Uproar is racket,
Racket is turmoil,
Turmoil is pandemonium
And that is a . . .
                    hullabaloo!

Sarah Liddell (10)
Cragside Primary School

THE SCHOOL HALL

I walked into the school hall,
You'll never guess what I saw,
A big, smashing party and a huge food stall,
They danced and danced, a hullabaloo!
I never believed that's what they'd do.

The food was all wacky
And the people were bonkers,
There was even a stall selling some conkers!
I looked round and round, trying not to be sick,
But someone suddenly gave me a kick!

That little hit changed my life from then on,
I started to party like never before,
The party had ended, everybody was gone,
I was last out and I shut the door.
Life's a hullabaloo!

Rishi Kohli (11)
Cragside Primary School

HOMEWORK, HOMEWORK

Homework, homework, always the same,
Sometimes good but mostly a pain.

Maths, science, history, art,
Keep us busy, keep us smart.

Victorians, Romans, Egyptians, Jews,
Look on the web to find some news.

There's no time to sing and play,
Because it's homework, homework, every day.

So teachers please don't bother us,
Or we'll run about and make a fuss.

Claire Bentham (10)
Cragside Primary School

FOOD FIGHT

The tomato from the kitchen
Splattered on the floor.
Cooks sitting in wonder,
To see what is in store.

Soup on the Miss's head,
Veg on the seat,
Spicy carrot curry,
Even the sweet!

Chuck it at the bullies,
Chuck it at the young'uns,
Nothing can stop us,
Food fight with onions!

Laurie Dudley (10)
Cragside Primary School

ANIMALS

Cats scrap,
Bats flap,
Horses neigh,
Puppies play,
Wolves howl,
Foxes growl,
Cows munch,
Rabbits crunch,
Sheep bleat,
Birds tweet,
Lions roar
And seagulls soar.

Sarah Henderson (10)
Cragside Primary School

THE UGLY-EYED MONSTER

Bats, cats and lots of rats
The mountain's tumbling
My tummy's rumbling.
Dogs, hogs and lots of frogs
In the pond you see him respond
Eyes like stars, junk off cars
Just remember things are near you
Just wait, he might say . . . *'Boo!'*

Ruby Catherall (9)
Cragside Primary School

IT WASN'T MY FAULT

It wasn't my fault, Miss,
I didn't know a robber would steal my RE
And when I chased him he shot me in the knee

It wasn't my fault, Sir,
I didn't even know aliens existed
But one came into my house
And lasered my homework to the top of a tree
I tried to stop it but it lasered me out to sea.

It wasn't my fault, Miss,
I didn't know my dog hadn't any tea
And would decide to eat my history
And when I tried to stop him, he bit my hand.

Peter Harrison (9)
Cragside Primary School

BEDTIME

At night I tuck my toys in
And make them warm for bed.
Then I lie myself down
And relax my sleepy head.

I get up and look in the mirror
And see my unforgetful eye.
I walk towards the window
And look into the darkest sky.

I get back into my bed,
Then count the white sheep,
But sooner or later,
I fall into a deep, dark sleep.

I just close my eyes,
That's how I get to sleep, me.
It is! It is!
And forever it will be.

Jacob Frame (9)
Cragside Primary School

THE PARK

During the hours of the dark,
A lonely girl wanders the park,
She tries to warm her freezing toes,
Kicking nature as she goes.

She carries on walking, on and on,
Until she reaches the duck pond,
For here she huddles in the leaves,
Whilst thinking of things she may need.

Eventually, when she falls asleep,
A man sees her in a ragged heap,
He shakes his head at the girl in her dreams
And thinks of all the others like her he's seen.

The old man sighs as he heads off to his home,
Though he does not want to leave the girl alone,
His feet feel heavy, though he does not know why,
What a way to live and die!

Sara Brignall (10)
Cragside Primary School

CREATURES OF THE WORLD

Hopping through the outback,
Searching is little Joey,
Hunting in the north,
A polar bear, white and snowy.

Fishing in the south,
A penguin, white and black,
The tiger in the jungle,
Longing for a tasty snack.

From its shiny, silky web,
The spider's catching flies,
The fox hungry for more,
In waiting he lies.

Creatures of the world,
Surviving day by day,
Living with great fear,
Becoming another's prey.

Anthony Sidney (10)
Cragside Primary School

BLUE SKY

The sky is like a big blue sheet floating like balloons
The rain is like someone crying in the clouds.

A plant is like a human growing as tall as a sunflower
As I stand beneath the boughs and stare up in the sky.

Here I am in the night with the stars and the moon
But the sun has come to die.

But we all know that the sun is hot and all is bright
But we all know that the sun said, 'Bye!'

Daniel Bailey (11)
Cragside Primary School

My Dog

I have a dog,
She is quite big.
She plays in the garden,
She likes to dig.

Her name is Gypsy,
And she is ten,
She comes in my bedroom,
Every now and then.

When she barks,
I get a fright,
She keeps me awake,
All through the night.

In the morning,
I let her out,
She is very funny,
She runs about.

She loves her bones,
She loves to chew,
And even sometimes,
Chews a shoe.

She eats her food,
Then goes to bed,
But she would rather
Play outside instead.

Roshelle Roche (10)
Cragside Primary School

THE UNUSUAL CAT

Once there was a cat
that never moved off the mat,

I forgot to tell you that
he lived in a two-storey flat,

It is unusual that a spotty old cat
lived in a flat,

But then he saw a rat
and he thought of a nice tasty dinner.

Rosemary Hind (10)
Cragside Primary School

FOOTBALL FANTASTIC

F ast and furious
O n the ball,
O bstacle-jumping
T iming it all.
B eating the opponent
A ll the way to the goal,
L ook and it's in the net
L ove it, it's a goal.

F ootie is the best
A nd so it should be,
N othing can stop it
T ill it comes to me.
A nd if you want a challenge
S how me what you have got,
T he net is waiting there
I t wants your shot.
C ome on, football, it needs you,
Because it isn't really
Anything new.

Ashley Frame (11)
Cragside Primary School

FOOTBALL CRAZY

Welcome to this football match
We promise a great show,
We've Shearer, Figo, Giggsy too
And don't forget Ronaldo.

We await the kick-off
There the whistle blasts,
It's Shearer, Shearer, all the way
Blimey, is he fast?

'Shearer, Shearer, Shearer, Shearer,'
The crowd chants joyfully,
We're running down the pitch again
Arrgghh! He nearly made it three!

We're counting down the seconds
Please don't let them score,
Come on Ref, blow your whistle
I can't take this anymore.

Matthew Payne (10)
Cragside Primary School

THE FLICK, FLACK

Bobby hates to be let down when Dyer plays in his dressing gown,
Standing still half-asleep, the ball comes at his face
Beep! Beep!
Robert shoots, hits the bar, blames that dude, Lua Lua,
Loses control of the ball, runs and down a ditch he falls.

Goes to the ref, talks at pace, Ref is cheeky, 'Shut your face!'
In the net, Lua Lua, it's in the back and here comes his famous
Flick, flack!

Jack Dennett (10)
Cragside Primary School

RAT FACE

His eyes are mean.
He's really keen.
His tail is like a worm
Which makes me squirm.
His body is grey
And he never sees the light of day.

He lives in the sewer, dark and damp
But he only appears when I turn on my bedroom lamp.
His grisly shadow always looks at me
And when I stand up very tall,
I realise he's only a patch on my wall.

Joshua Hornby (11)
Cragside Primary School

BUSY BEE!

They are stripy
Orange and black,
They have fuzzy hair
On their back.

They live in a hive
And make lots of honey,
They have big eyes
And I think they look funny!

Busy bee, busy bee,
You are as happy as can be.

Adam Dillon (8)
Cragside Primary School

ORANGES

Oranges,
Pears,
Peaches,
Plums,
Do you like them?
Yum! Yum!

Apples
Kiwi, lemon, gum
I like them
But the best is gum!

Sam MacGregor (8)
Cragside Primary School

TOWNS AND FARMS

The sky is blue,
The clouds are grey,
The cows go 'Moo!'
The horse goes 'Neigh.'

The rubbish in the street,
The rats in the bins,
The people the rats meet,
And all the metal tins.

The paper in the gutters,
All of the lost toys,
All the mumbly mutters,
And the naughty girls and boys.

Kerry-Anne Browne (9)
Cragside Primary School

EAGLE DIVE

Eagle dive
Eagle j
      u   p
       m
Eagle hop, hop, fall, fall,
Bump.

Owly skip,
Owly j   m
      u   p
Owly skip, skip, hop, hop,
Thump.

Vulture trip
Vulture j
        Um
            p
Vulture trip, trip, plip, plop
Flump.

Nicole MacGregor (11)
Cragside Primary School

PANIC

Panic is the colour of grey, like vicious gas booming
out of the shower nozzles and bringing innocent
people to their deaths.

It tastes like sweet lemon, tingling the back of your throat,
making you constantly cough on and on and on.

It smells like someone's rotting body lying in a furnace
waiting to be cremated.

It feels like someone's drowning you with their bare hands
and enjoying it while it lasts.

It sounds like the hissing of the gas, squirting out of every way out.

It lives in the heart of the afraid.

Paul Fradgley ((10)
Delaval Primary School

WITCHES' BREW

Double, double, toil and trouble,
Fire burn and cauldron bubble.
Bat's wing, rotten brains,
Lizard swing in the drains.
Witches' cauldrons - mixing spells
Witches flying, pungent smells.
Add a pumpkin without a sound,
Mixing, mixing, round and round.
Double, double, toil and trouble,
Fire burn and cauldron bubble.
Spider's leg, people dying,
Snake's skin, bats flying.

Lee Ray (10)
Delaval Primary School

MAIDEN RAIN

The rain is a maiden,
Weeping at her woes,
Tears down her face,
Shivers at her toes.

Her face is at your window,
She's tapping at the pane,
She's tiptoeing on the roof,
She's lying in the lane.

But here's a smile,
It's all across her face,
She packs up her woes,
And takes them to another place.

Lauren Rolph (11)
Kingston Park Primary School

SULLEY AND SPOT

I knew a cat called Sulley
Who really was a big bully
He was as big as a mat
And mean and fat
That horrible cat, Sulley.

Sulley had a friend called Spot
And they hung around quite a lot
When they came out to play
All the cats went away
Those awful cats, Sulley and Spot.

Along came a girl called Dot
Who didn't like Sulley or Spot
She gave them a clout
That sorted them out
That was the last you saw of Sulley or Spot.

Charlotte Gilroy (9)
La Sagesse Junior School

THE END OF THE WORLD IS NEAR

The end of the world is near
I am sure, sure, sure,
And it's not a pretty sight.
There are werewolves jumping
Vampires are sucking!
The ghost trains will never be the same
One ghost got on, three boys got on
And were never seen again.
The end of the world has come for me,
I am banned from watching my TV!

Emma Donohoe (8)
La Sagesse Junior School

MY SPECIAL PET, LUCY

Playing in the garden outside
The leaves are all around us
Shuffling, rolling and sniffing
She plays along all day.

Wind blows through the air
Ruffling her hair
Tired, the next day
She goes to sleep.

Then I haven't got anyone to play with
Then, fit and healthy the next day
Fit and ready to go
Then she goes back to sleep.
Oh well!

Lisa Chambers (9)
La Sagesse Junior School

MY DAD

My dad is the best,
My dad beats all the rest,
He is funny and very clever,
But lazy is one thing he is, never.

I wake up and he is away.
Starting with a 12-mile run for the day,
Then comes home to take us out on our bikes,
Sport is what he really likes.

He trains not just for fun,
Every day it has to be done,
Swimming, cycling and a run,
To be an 'iron man' this has to be done!

That is why my dad is different from the rest,
Yes, he is definitely the best!

Charlotte Hudson (8)
La Sagesse Junior School

THE MAN WHO WILL MARRY ME

On Fantasy Island over the sea,
There might be a man who'll marry me,
He could be thin,
He could be tall,
He could be fat,
He could be small.
He might not even be there at all,
The man who'll marry me.

In a dense green jungle far away,
There might be a man who'll come and stay.
He could be rich,
He could be free,
Maybe he'll ask to marry me.
He may not even be there at all,
The man who'll marry me.

Eleanor Reynolds (9)
La Sagesse Junior School

GET OUT THE DOOR

Get out the door on a Friday night,
Move to the music, dance all night,
Mum drinks wine, I drink Coke,
The music is too fast for Dad to cope.
Time to get home before it's too late,
Or my dad may have a date,
Get in the car,
Off we go!

Megan Roberts (9)
La Sagesse Junior School

MY ROOM

My room is messy all the time
My mum says, 'Tidy it.'
I say, 'It's fine.'
I thought of tidying it
But I just did a little bit.
I told my mum I'd do it soon
After all it is my room.

In my room I keep my diary,
Bags, gloves and CD - Kylie.
Also I keep my precious things,
Glitter balls and my rings.
My toys are lying on the floor
I play with them for evermore.
I know I'll be told, 'Tidy the floor.'
So I hide them all behind the door.

Amelia Armstrong (9)
La Sagesse Junior School

MY PET RABBIT

I have a pet rabbit
She lives at the bottom of my garden
I love her very much
She lives in a hutch
I feed her carrots and broccoli
She eats it very fast
I love to play with her
But she just runs and hops away
She has white fluffy ears
And a white fluffy tail
Can you guess her name?
Her name is *Fluffy!*

Sarah Gourley (7)
La Sagesse Junior School

MY PET HAMSTER

Every time I go to see my hamster
She always runs away
She hides in the corner of her cage
And nibbles at her food.
When she turns around
Her pouches are full to bursting
When she goes to bed
She puts her food in too
And eats it during the night.
In the morning
My hamster is on her wheel
My brother gives her a fright
Because he flicks on the light.

Caroline Dixon (8)
La Sagesse Junior School

MY RABBIT

I have a little rabbit,
He is very, very cute,
He has some little mittens
And a rather little suit,
I sometimes put a little bow
In his furry little hair,
I fill him with some laughter
And lots and lots of care.
He loves to eat, he loves to play,
His little bear is made of clay.
That is my rabbit, I love him a lot!

Ciara McFaul (8)
La Sagesse Junior School

I HAD A FRIEND

I had a friend
But now he's gone
Oh, I wish he were here
But he's not
I hope I will see him again
But if I don't
I doubt I will
Have a friend like Sam again
But if I do,
Yahoo, see you!

Scarlett Coles (8)
La Sagesse Junior School

LEAVES

Leaves here
Leaves there
There are leaves everywhere
Leaves in the back garden
Leaves in the front garden
Red, yellow, orange, brown,
Soon the leaves will come tumbling down.

Jessica Fulgenzi (8)
La Sagesse Junior School

MY MONSTER SISTER

My monster sister is a monster
She is so naughty and nasty
She is so, so creepy
She sneaks up on me and scares me
I jump out of my skin.

I tell ya, I tell ya,
She is a monster
She nearly tried to eat me!
Believe me, she is a real
Monster!

Lara Allen (7)
La Sagesse Junior School

MIDNIGHT MOON

The clock strikes twelve
The moon grows bright
The house is dark with shadows
And then in creeps the light

It covers every little object
Over all the fading curtains
It creeps over all the antique chairs
And wakes the ghost up in her lair

Then she wakes and strokes her hound
She checks the house all over twice
She stares out at the twilight garden
Her eyes are as cold as ice

She opens up a room
That has no light nor window
Only the ghostly midnight moon
And a small candle

In that room she takes a book
And reads a page in whisper
No one else has had a look
So no one knows how she disappears

The clock strikes one
The moon grows dull
The house returns to shadows.

Francesca Ayre (10)
La Sagesse Junior School

TOON ARMY

Every Saturday I join the Toon Army,
Marching up on St James' Park.
Jostling crowds all going barmy
Hoping their heroes make their mark.

Taking my seat, I look around
At the black, white and green of the football ground.
Thousands of people, small as ants,
The roar of the crowd singing their chants.

The pitch is enormous, so bright and so green,
The teams run out, so glad to be seen,
Black and white against the red and white enemy,
                                    an awesome sight!

For 45 minutes we cheer and shout,
As the half-time whistle blows, we fight to get out.
In the bar for chips and Coke,
A welcome break despite the smoke.

The second half begins with the score at one-nil,
A cross from Dyer, Shearer puts it in the back of the net,
Two-nil it remains, the fans have had their fill,
Another result! We'll win the league yet!

Katie Crumbley (10)
La Sagesse Junior School

SUNSET

A noisy beach
a jam-packed pool
soaking up the summer sun!

Clouds are covering
our favourite star!
'Come back out.'
'We're staying where we are!'

A quiet beach,
an empty pool
they gave up on the sun
as it set into the west.

Lucy O'Donnell (10)
La Sagesse Junior School

THE LUCKY PINK BUTTON

I was walking down the stairs from a lesson
and I found a pink button,
how very odd, maybe it's lucky,
I picked it up and slipped it in my pocket.

It was there all day
and when we came to do a test
it was really easy, it was the best.

I took it to my lessons
and worked really hard
I took it to French
and got a gold star.

I took it to a netball match
and gosh, we won 7-3!
That button's really lucky
but for no one else but me!

Beth Watson (11)
La Sagesse Junior School

NETBALL

'Offside! Careful Lakshmi, you go . . . footwork!'
Boring! Come on then!

'High shot, Eram! Come on girls. Middles!'
The ball's never coming up here.

I wish Beth would stop shooting.
I hope Eleanor will go slow.
I want Eram to shrink just a little bit.
I need the ball up near this goal.

I've been standing here for ages.
Beth and Eram keep on shooting.
They're really just too fast for me.
We're running circles round the other team.

Eram's speed really won the match.
Well, Beth did also help, I suppose.
Eleanor, dashing and dodging, did as well.
Mrs Bartram helped with shooting
The odd time or two or three over the years!

Claire Allen (10)
La Sagesse Junior School

VALENTINE'S DAY

Valentine's Day is about
hearts and love
teddies, sweets and cuddly toys.

Valentine's Day means
soppy poems,
flowers, gifts and cards.

Valentine's Day is about
reading loved ones' cards and verses
and admiring them one by one.

Valentine's Day means all the
sweetest things
like 'roses are red, violets are blue'
and 'be my valentine'.

Philippa Mulgrove (11)
La Sagesse Junior School

THE THINGS I LIKE TO DO BEST!

Reading is so relaxing
Reading is so enjoyable
Reading is so entertaining
It's what I like to do best.

Swimming is so exhausting
Swimming is so tiring
Swimming is so great
It's what I like to do best.

Drawing is so artistic
Drawing is so creative
Drawing is so exciting
It's what I like to do best.

Bike riding is so adventurous
Bike riding is so mysterious
Bike riding is so cool
It's what I like to do best.

Horse riding is so interesting
Horse riding is so amazing
Horse riding is so elegant
It's what I like to do best.

Jessica Bell (10)
La Sagesse Junior School

HULLABALOO

At the starting line we will start
On our bikes we shall start
Will we fly into space
Or shall we stay and race?

On the rings of Saturn
Gliding on our bikes
Zooming through the galaxy
On our Saturn bikes.

Charlotte Bennetts (11)
La Sagesse Junior School

BIRTHDAYS

Birthdays are fun
Birthdays are funny
Sometimes if you're lucky
You might get some money.
Bake a cake
Jam and cream
Hear the children shout and scream.
Blow your candles and make a wish.
Don't forget to close your eyes
I hope you get a nice surprise!

Happy birthday!

Lee Summers (11)
St Mark's RC Primary School, Westerhope

AUTUMN

Brown, red and orange, turn the leaves
As they fall from the big trees above.
Crunch, crisp, crinkle, as I walk
Sounds like the leaves can talk.
Shh!

Laura Simpson (10)
St Mark's RC Primary School, Westerhope

THAT DAY IN NOVEMBER

I love bonfires and fireworks.
Freezing dark scary nights.
Flying lights.
Smoking is billowing,
Orange, red and yellow.
I remember
That day in November.

James Roberts (11)
St Mark's RC Primary School, Westerhope

AUTUMN

I walk down the street
And the night is colder.
The leaves are brown,
They are a season older.

Autumn has come,
The trees become bare.
The leaves fall on the ground,
As if they lose their hair.

Autumn is the season
I like best.
It is closer to winter,
Then Christmas is next.

Ross Minto (11)
St Mark's RC Primary School, Westerhope

MY GUITAR

When I'm older, I'll be a star,
Playing tunes on my guitar,
People will come from miles around,
To listen to my beautiful sound,
I'll strike some chords, pluck some strings,
Add a tune or words or things.
I'll play the music every day,
'That's going to be a hit,' they will say.
Then when I'm famous, the money I'll bank,
It's Mam and Dad I'll have to thank
For the Christmas present of an electric guitar,
Which made their son a well-known star!

Sam Monkhouse (11)
St Mark's RC Primary School, Westerhope

AUTUMN

Autumn arrives
And there are no longer blue skies,
There are no sunrays
On these cold windy days,
The green leaves turn to brown
As they fall to the ground,
The flowers disappear,
Autumn is here.

Stephanie Corbett (10)
St Mark's RC Primary School, Westerhope

DINOSAURS
(A haiku)

Dinosaurs were huge
They could be big as a house
But now they're extinct!

Liam Collins (10)
St Mark's RC Primary School, Westerhope

NEWCASTLE UNITED

Newcastle United are the best of them all
they're quick, they're fast, they're on the ball.

Shearer's the captain of the team,
he's sleek and tall and mean and lean.

Bobby Robson manages the best,
he keeps his team above the rest.

The goalkeeper stands tall on his line,
Shay Given keeps the goals out time after time.

The rest of the team are all so great,
keeping the crowd coming through the gate!

Lucy Potts (8)
St Mark's RC Primary School, Westerhope

WHEN SHEARER SCORES

When Shearer scores
Sir Bobby jumps out of the dugout
Shay Given swings on his goalpost
And the Toon Army cheer.

When Shearer scores
Kieron Dyer gives him a big hug
Fans kiss each other
And some spill their beer.

When Shearer scores
He doesn't do a Lua Lua flip
He doesn't stand on Craig Bellamy's toes
He just puts his hand in the air.

That's why Shearer and Newcastle are my heroes.

Autumn Irving-Carr (8)
St Mark's RC Primary School, Westerhope

MISS WADE

Our teacher is Miss Wade,
She was born to amaze,
She makes us do as she says,
So the poem says.

Our teacher, Miss Wade,
Is one in a billion,
She teaches us maths
And we count to one million.

She teaches us lessons
And teaches us spellings
That we want to learn,
We all get the message when Miss Wade is quite stern.

St Mark's is our school,
It's one of the best,
We play in the yard,
Then soon have a rest.

Sophie Monaghan (8)
St Mark's RC Primary School, Westerhope

BONFIRE NIGHT

Once a year in early November,
We enjoy a day to remember,
With fireworks bright and fires hot,
We all celebrate the gunpowder plot.

Callum Rankin (10)
St Mark's RC Primary School, Westerhope

THAT DAY

I took a bus
to Tynemouth Bay,
it was not long,
I spent the day.

I fell into a ditch,
once I got all the prickles out,
I soon had a drink of rum.

I soon got warm,
and took a splash,
into the lovely water,
it was glimmering out of sight,
but then it came back in,
I got so wet,
I soon became cold.

It was time to go home,
it was quite dark,
I soon knew that I would
go back to Tynemouth Bay
another day.

Debra Webb (11)
St Mark's RC Primary School, Westerhope

ABE'S UNDERWORLD

On a different planet far away
Lived a Mudukon named Abe
Skin of blue, three-fingered hands and boneless toes.
Large glowing eyes as bright as the sun,
With a wrinkly bulbous nose.
To save the Mudukons from soulstorm brew,
Was his destiny.

Scrabs and Paramites, slogs and sligs,
Fleeches and Glokens too.
These were the ones who turned Mudukons into soulstorm brew.
If you look hard to outer space,
You are bound to see
That dark polluted, needed place . . .

Oddworld!

Sean Nickerson (10)
St Mark's RC Primary School, Westerhope

I AM MISSING MY DAD

I am missing my dad
because he's not here
he works away
day after day.
When he comes back
we have a meal
and enjoy the good news
that he is here.

I miss his smile
and his happy face,
when he comes home
he brightens the place.

Oh God, if you will
listen to me,
don't let him
ever forget me!

Lucy Marshall (11)
St Mark's RC Primary School, Westerhope

GOALKEEPERS

Daniel is my name
To be a goalkeeper is my aim
I like to pounce and catch the ball
At that I am good because I'm quite tall
But at least in most lessons I'm not a teacher's pet.
At least I'm good at stopping the ball hitting the net,
Just like Kirkland, my idol, whom I hope to meet,
But I have met Shearer and his amazing pair of striking feet!
As you guess and I hope you see
A goalkeeper is the dream for me.
Being a goalkeeper is my need
And at that I hope and know I'll do my best to succeed!

Daniel Mullen (11)
St Mark's RC Primary School, Westerhope

THE MAGIC PURSE

Inside the magic purse is a secret,
It might be . . .
A golden coin jumping,
A sparkling gel pen writing brightly,
A rainbow smiling happily.
We don't know, the secret is locked inside!

Slobodan Aleksic (8)
St Paul's CE Primary School, Elswick

THE MAGIC PURSE

Inside the magic purse is a secret
It might be . . .
A rich necklace shining like a star
A golden bracelet shining like angels
A magnet shimmering brightly
A rusty bracelet rolling gently
An elegant rainbow shooting through the sky
A sparkling frozen leaf getting blown away
A golden key spinning around
A glass bottle noisily clanking
A lily pad sitting lazily on the pond.

These are the sweet charms
I think are inside the magic purse.

Naomi Mirza (8)
St Paul's CE Primary School, Elswick

THE MAGIC PURSE

Inside the magic purse
Is a secret
It might be . . .
A sparkling bracelet breaking easily
A helpless mouse dying slowly
A golden egg spinning smoothly
A silvery ball rolling gently
A fierce tiger attacking quickly
A baby boy crying quietly
We don't know
The secret is locked
Safe inside!

Lee-Edward Lee (9)
St Paul's CE Primary School, Elswick

MY FAMILY

My nanna is old
My grandad is bold.

My aunties are rough
My uncles are tough.

My mam's a bit crazy
My dad is very lazy.

Georgia Chambers (10)
St Paul's CE Primary School, Elswick

DREAMS

I lay on my back in the long grass.
The birds were singing overhead.
The first thing I knew, I was dreaming.
That's when I rolled out of my bed!

Samantha Brown (10)
St Paul's CE Primary School, Elswick

THE HOMELESS MAN

There were people walking down the street
What did they see?
They saw a person, homeless and sweet
Picking crumbs up from the gardens and street
Trying to keep warm with a paper sheet.
As he cried himself to sleep
They ran down to wake him up
He woke up with a frown
And dropped to the ground with his eyes closed!

Stephanie Hawman (11)
St Paul's CE Primary School, Elswick

STARS

Stars are fast, stars are slow,
Do they go high, or do they go low?
Stars look over you when you sleep at night,
They guide you with their special light.
Stars are busy at night, swirling, whirling,
Dancing and prancing.
Stars are yellow and never change,
But if they were blue, they would still care for you.

Jade Allan (11)
St Paul's CE Primary School, Elswick

THE MAGIC PURSE

Inside the magic purse is a secret
It might be . . .
A silver sparkling key waiting to get touched
A fiery dragon blowing fire
A sparkling ring rolling gently
A shimmering jewel spinning with delight
A magic fairy waving her wand beautifully
A genie granting a wish grumpily
A rainbow covered with jewels brightly.
I don't know.
The secret is locked safe inside.

Chelsea Francis (8)
St Paul's CE Primary School, Elswick

THE MAGIC PURSE

Inside the magic purse
Is a secret
It might be . . .
A shimmering ring rolling gracefully,
A golden necklace sparkling brightly,
A silver earring spinning quickly,
A colourful button spinning slowly,
A golden lamp with a sparkling genie.
We don't know,
The secret is locked inside the purse.

Charlotte Gibson (8)
St Paul's CE Primary School, Elswick

Music Beat

Out of all the different music, I like pop,
I stand in my room and bop.
   Singsong! Singsong!

There are disco rooms and ballrooms,
Singing witches on brooms,
A fast car with loud music zooms.
   Singsong! Singsong!

Know the words, sing along,
The rock music drums going *bong!*
   Singsong! Singsong!

Rock bands, pop bands all doing a . . .
   Singsong! Singsong!

Racheal Woods (10)
St Paul's CE Primary School, Elswick

HEADACHE

I wake up in my bed
Everything I see looks red.

I've got a funny feeling in my head.

Teacher always shouting,
Kids always pouting.

I've got a funny feeling in my head.

Little sister crying,
Feel like I'm dying.

I've got a funny feeling in my head.

I take a pill to relieve the pain,
But it just drives me insane.

I've got a funny feeling in my head.

Rhys Ansah (9)
St Paul's CE Primary School, Elswick

HOORAY THE BOO! POEM

They're pulling the old school down. *Hooray!*
And building a new one in its place. *Boo!*
There'll be no hard work. *Hooray!*
Because it'll be solid work. *Boo!*
We won't finish at three. *Hooray!*
We will never finish. *Boo!*
We won't have a small playground. *Hooray!*
We'll have a titchy playground. *Boo!*
There'll be no more horrible veg. *Hooray!*
There's no dinner at all. *Boo!*
It won't be a big school. *Hooray!*
It'll be a gigantic school. *Boo!*
The school holidays start today. *Hooray!*
And end in 10 minutes. *Boo!*
You don't have to wear a school uniform. *Hooray!*
We won't be wearing anything! *Boo!*

Kevin Stobbs (8)
St Paul's CE Primary School, Elswick

FLOWERS

Flowers are beautiful
And as tall as towers,
They sway as the wind goes by.

Flowers link and blink,
Flowers come in pink,
They dance in the sun.

Flowers are small,
Flowers are colourful,
Flowers are bright.

Flowers talk in the sun,
Flowers dance in the wind.

Flowers are wild,
Flowers are thin,
Flowers are fat,
And so beautiful and tame.

Holly Amanda Cheshire (10)
Whickham Parochial School

AT THE SEASIDE

At the seaside it is hot and cold
Down on the sand ice cream is sold.

At the seaside people have fun
Playing on the beach and lazing in the sun.

At the seaside, children run wild
Building sandcastles and jumping with the tide.

At the seaside I love to be
As there's so much to do and see.

Rebecca Holdsworth (9)
Whickham Parochial School

FOOTBALL

I love playing football,
It fills me with cheer.
I like scoring goals,
I have no fear.

I like to slide around
And love getting muddy.
Passing the ball,
To my teammate, Buddy.

I hate getting tackled,
Or getting a kick.
If it's really bad,
It can make you feel sick.

I run around,
Kicking the ball.
Sometimes I have
A nasty fall.

When I'm in goal,
I like to save
And I celebrate
By giving a wave.

Newcastle United,
Is the team I like most.
They often score,
But they sometimes hit the post.

I walk to St James'
And as I get nearer,
I dream of goals
Scored by Alan Shearer.

Daniel Bainbridge (9)
Whickham Parochial School

THE CAVEMAN

In a dark cave late at night
A caveman sat out of sight
Watching the stars and moon in the sky
He saw some bats flying by.

In a dark cave late at night
A caveman lay asleep out of sight
He dreamed of a wonderland far away
With rolling hills on a summery day.

In a dark cave late at night
A caveman sat by the firelight
He wondered why he was all alone
And hoped one day he could go back home.

In a dark cave late at night
A caveman watched the moon so bright
Thinking of his family sadly
He would return to them gladly.

Amber Rundle (10)
Whickham Parochial School

SPOT

There once was a cat called Spot
Who always slept on my bed
He purred on his plot
As he lay on my head

He was a very hungry cat
Eating everything in sight
Having tried to catch a bat
It made him very light

Spot became so, so thin
As he dreamed of eating fish
Jumping from bin to bin
He realised it was his empty dish

Spot woke up with a fright
To find there were no bats
As it was the middle of the night
All he found were cats.

Emma Patterson (10)
Whickham Parochial School

BODIES AND BRAINS

Tall and thin, small and round
Differing bodies are abound
Be thee large, be thee small,
The brain inside differs in all
Some are bright, some are not
It does not matter if they give their lot.

Jack Gibson (9)
Whickham Parochial School

THE BEST CAT, AND THAT'S THAT!

Ginger is the best cat in the world
Well at least I think that.
I am James
And Ginger is my cat.

I will tell you about Ginger
And other types of cat
And I'm going to tell you
Just like that!

A few of the verses
Are going to rhyme
But it's not going to rhyme
All of the time!

There are over 100 different breeds
From pale to bold colours
From the Red Persian
To orange tabbies.

Some cats have long hair,
Some have short.
Rough or smooth,
What's your favourite sort?

Cats and dogs
Really don't get along
Cats are fast
And dogs are strong.

Cats usually go up trees
They get away from the dog with ease!

Ginger's favourite food is rabbit,
When I open the pouch
He just tries to grab it!

I think Ginger's the best cat,
The poem's at an end
And that is that!

James Matthew Williams (9)
Whickham Parochial School

FRIENDS

Friends are so special
Nice and kind
They always think twice about what's on their mind
They never think bad of the things that you do
They're always around and there for you.

Amy Hails (10)
Whickham Parochial School

ALAN SHEARER

He's got skill
And is full of will
And all for his team, United!

He grabs a couple,
Because he's so supple
And all for his team, United!

He takes free kicks
And he's full of tricks
And all for his team, United!

He's our penalty-taker
And he is a playmaker
And all for his team, United!

He loses his defender
And is sometimes an offender
And all for his team, United!

He unites his team
And the cup is his dream
And all for his team, United!
Yes, all for his team, United!

Alexander McGregor (10)
Whickham Parochial School

THE SUN

The sun is a star that shines so bright
It shines during the day but not at night
The sun is a great source of vitamin D
You'll feel good, look good, for everyone to see
But please beware, it can go wrong
The sun can burn if you're in it too long.

Kieran Tong (9)
Whickham Parochial School

SWEET ANIMALS!

Animals are like sweets,
Some soft, some hard,
Some big, some small.

Giraffes with long Fudge bar necks,
Fluffy marshmallow polar bears,
Monkeys' tails are liquorice strings,
Elephants' bodies like big Double Deckers.

Cool penguins remind me of Polo mints,
Humbugs like stripy tigers,
Birds, the colours of fruit gums.

That's how I see animals,
Do you?

Sarah Bilton (10)
Whickham Parochial School

My Family And How They Make Me Feel

My mam is always there,
She's full of love and tender care.
She's always there without a thought,
Giving me lots of support.

I miss my dad when he's away,
Because we always laugh and play,
When he's home I feel so glad,
That's why he's the greatest dad.

My sister plays her music loud,
But even so she makes me proud,
It's great being sisters for one another,
It's much better than having a brother.

I have a little guinea pig called Connie,
She's black and white and really bonny,
She runs and plays, but prefers to eat,
So every day I make her a special treat.

My family means everything to me,
It's got everything a family needs to be,
Every day is full of love, joy and fun
Now I think my poem is done.

Olivia Holness (10)
Whickham Parochial School

OH NO!

My mum comes home, she slams the door
It's not long before we hear a roar.
The music is loud, the room's a mess,
'Now boys, stop playing chess.'
She enters the room, her face turns red
'Get ready boys, it looks like we're dead.'
She growls and groans and stares at me,
'It's my brother's fault,
Can't you see?'
She bellows and shouts and throws things around
The boys stay silent not making a sound.
She flusters and blusters and makes herself hoarse
Then loses her voice and that's the end of course.

Hannah Elizabeth Boath (9)
Whickham Parochial School

The Day Of The Hogwarts Storm

I had a big breakfast to fill up my tum
Before travelling to see Auntie Joan down in Brum
I left the Toon station, my hopes riding high
Dreams of witchcraft and broomsticks and learning to fly.

Two days with my aunt who I don't often see
Then a trip down to Hogwarts will be magic for me
My auntie is funny and brilliant at cooking
She gives me dark chocolate when no one is looking

The Hogwarts Express was to leave about ten
But stuttered and stalled and did not move then
It was pouring with rain and there were trees on the track
There was no going forward and no going back

The weather got wetter and colder, not hotter
This day can't be saved, not *even* by Potter!
No witchcraft, wizardry or Quidditch at all
Not even my cream tea in the Great Hall

The advert had said 'Ride the Hogwarts Express,
Who could have known it would be such a mess?
Back home to my aunt's, a long journey ahead
I think when I get there I'll go straight to bed!

Daniel Fairlamb (9)
Whickham Parochial School

FLORIDA

Hot sun is burning down,
Soon I will be pink and brown.
I'm so excited to be here,
Visiting the mouse with the famous ears!

Roller coasters, fun to watch,
But sometimes scary to ride.
When I'm at the very top
I always close my eyes.

I love to splash in the water parks
And go on all the rides.
You have to be brave
For some of the big slides.

Florida is great!

Emma Falcus (10)
Whickham Parochial School

POP STARS

Instruments are playing,
Hips are swaying.
Pop stars on the stage.
Their clothes are all the rage.
Pink is on the go,
Dancing to and fro!

Ellen Wood (8)
Whickham Parochial School

SILLY SAMMY SHARK AND CATCHY CROCODILE

Silly Sammy Shark swam through the
water hunting for his lunch,
when he met a crocodile called Catch.
Catchy Crocodile was looking for his
friend, he wanted to play catch.
Sammy Shark and Catchy Crocodile
became best friends and swam
together every day, playing
hide-and-seek and having lots of fun.

Andrew Wharton (8)
Whickham Parochial School

HOLIDAY BLUES

I went to Spain on holiday,
Rushed to the pool to dive. *Hooray!*
You'll never guess what happened to me,
I dived into the pool and bashed my knee.
My mam, my dad, they laughed at me
Arrgghh! My rotten family!
I'll get my revenge, just wait and see!

Jake Sturrock (7)
Whickham Parochial School

MR LEAF

Mr Leaf on the tree,
are you talking to me?

I can hear you rustling from way up there,
come to me, if you dare.

Now you fall down to the ground,
where you will be safe, safe and sound.

Kathryn Rutherford (7)
Whickham Parochial School

VALENTINE'S DAY

V alentine's Day is a time to celebrate
A happy day for someone you love
L ove can be very special for you
E veryone can love other people
N o one can resist a person you love
T rue love is all around on Valentine's Day
I n love and together
N ow is the time to celebrate
E veryone is happy at last.

Megan Peterson (7)
Whickham Parochial School

DANIEL

Daniel, my brother, is younger than me.
He's three, annoying and never eats his tea.
I was excited when he was born, he looked like Alan Shearer,
He's been around for so long, his voice is getting clearer.
Shouts orders around the house, he's like an army major.
He's Superman, Spider-Man and Buzz with a laser.
Although he spoils nearly everything,
I would not swap him for anything.

Iain Nicholson (8)
Whickham Parochial School

FOOTBALL

Football is my favourite sport
I watch it and play it all the time.
I love to wear my football strip,
Newcastle United are the best.
Shearer runs up the pitch, tackling as he goes,
Then he reaches the other net and scores a goal.
When I grow up I would like to be a footballer
And would like to be the captain of the team.

Christopher Neve (8)
Whickham Parochial School

MY BIKE

The wheels are spinning very fast
the colours blur and the drink handle wobbles.
When I am going too fast I have to pull my brakes
and when I go up hills I have to turn my gears.
I have to wear a helmet to keep me safe.
When I turn, I pull the handles to go in that direction
and to make me go I need to push the pedals with my feet.
Sometimes I lift myself off the seat and stand
and when people are in my way I ring my bell.

Matthew Neve (8)
Whickham Parochial School

NATURE

It's a nice sunny day
when I like to play
when the wind blows hard
in my backyard.

Branches falling
wind still calling
flowers that bloom
with spring so soon

Lots of dogs
sitting on logs
playing with balls
bouncing on walls

When I like to play
on a nice sunny day
I have so much fun
that I like to run.

Emily Miller (8)
Whickham Parochial School

THE RACEHORSE

There stood a horse
on the racecourse
he went racing away
towards the hay.

He knew he was hungry
by the rumble in his tummy
but when he got there
the manger was bare

He bucked and he kicked
and he went into a huff
but then he remembered
he was meant to be tough

Back to the course
in a blink of an eye
the race starter's gun
pointed up in the sky

Round and round
the horses did spin
every one of them
wanted to win

With a snort of his nose
and a whisk of his tail
our friend knew
that he must not fail

He won the race
but what was the prize?
A pile of hay,
what a nice surprise!

Sophie Loughlen (7)
Whickham Parochial School

MY SISTER

I have a little sister, she really is a pest.
She has blonde hair and big blue eyes
and always looks her best.
She likes the Tweenies and Blue's Clues
and loves to trash my room.
My first job when I come home from school
is to tidy up my bedroom.
So she may be a little tinker
and a great big pest
but I love her lots and lots.
She is the very best.
My sister!

Adam Lewis (7)
Whickham Parochial School

RHYMING DOGS

I have a dog, her name is Mog
She was out one day and saw a frog
Sitting on a log near a bog
My dog Mog picked up the log
And went for a jog near the bog
Down came the fog,
Mog dropped the log
And the frog jumped into the bog.

Jessica Hindson (7)
Whickham Parochial School

SOME MONTHS OF THE YEAR

One fine day,
Mrs May
Came along to make the sun shine!

Mr August,
Sent a big gust,
To make all the forecasters go wrong!

Mrs January,
Made Miss Kerry
Go quite around the U-bend!

Mr February,
Made a breeze quite airy,
It made everyone go quite crazy!

Mrs July,
Made my cousins, Alice and Amber,
Get hayfever!

Ellen Hayes (8)
Whickham Parochial School

WALKING TO SCHOOL IN THE SNOW

As I walk to school
I throw snowballs and have fun
I like the smell of winter
And the shining of the sun
I throw snowballs at my sister
I throw snowballs at my mum
I love walking to school in the morning
Because I have lots of fun.

Ruby Friel (8)
Whickham Parochial School

ABOUT AN ANIMAL

Animal, Animal, are you hurt?
I will see if you are marked.
You can come and live with me,
Animal, Animal, come with me
I will help you get better.
I love you, Animal.

Bethany Foster (8)
Whickham Parochial School

ALL ABOUT ME!

Poems you see,
Are a lot like me,
They can be short and sweet,
Or long and neat,
They can be about bananas,
Or even my warm pyjamas,
They can describe my favourite toys,
Or can be about boys,
Poems can be cool
While swimming in the pool,
They can be fantastic,
While doing gymnastics,
Now do you see
Why poems are just like me?

Rachel Farrey (8)
Whickham Parochial School

TV

TV. TV. TV.
Everyone loves TV.
There are films and shows
And everyone knows
Everyone loves TV.

TV. TV. TV.
Everyone loves TV.
Some films and shows
Are classified,
As being much too old for me!

TV. TV. TV.
Everyone loves TV.
But if you watch too much
You'll get square eyes
And not be able to see!

TV. TV. TV.
Everyone loves TV.
If you don't like it,
Put on your kit
And come and play football with me!

Joshua Crabtree (8)
Whickham Parochial School

MY BEST FRIEND, PEPPER

When I look in her brown eyes
I see her smiling back at me,
When I stroke her soft, velvety ears
I feel her close to me,
When I am sad
She comforts me,
When I am alone
She plays with me,
When I am naughty
She helps me!
When I am being silly
She's silly with me,
When I look at her picture
She's still here with me
Her big brown eyes - she smiles back at me!

Oliver Cooke (8)
Whickham Parochial School

FLIPPER, THE DOLPHIN

The big blue dolphins swim in the sea,
Over waves and jump with glee.
All of the fish say, 'Look out, Flipper's about!'
How I love to see dolphins swimming in the sea.
They jump around doing flips and tips.
My very favourite place to be is right here beside the sea.

Abby Cairns (7)
Whickham Parochial School

It's Snowball Time!

I like snow anywhere,
Falling on the ground,
Coming from the air,
It topples in a mound.

Miniature balls falling on my face,
They melt into water drops,
They are having a race,
When the flakes hit the ground, they pop!

When you get some snow,
You squash it with your hands,
You make a shape like an O,
Get ready to see where it lands!

Alexander Brissenden-Ruddy (7)
Whickham Parochial School

MY SISTER

My little sister, Lucy Boyle,
She's funny and juicy,
She has a little toy.
My grandad calls her Juicy Lucy.
Though often naughty, sometimes nice,
She's aged just three and nothing like me.

Elleanor Boyle (8)
Whickham Parochial School

AIRPORTS, PLANES AND YUCKY FOOD

When I was small, I looked in the sky.
Suddenly a plane went by.
Where will it go? I thought, *how does it stay,*
Up there with a trail of cloudy grey?

A trip to Heathrow, a really big jet
I found my answers, not all, just yet.
The pilot told me how it worked
I looked around inside and stared
Out of the window, wait, what's this?
I think she's called an air hostess.
'Would you like to eat?' she said,
'Yes please, my favourite, boiled eggs and bread.'
There's only this she said, as I got some slop
My excitement then began to stop.
The thrill of the plane disappeared, the fun
All I got was a manky bun!

Planes are great, airports too
But aircraft food - I need the loo!

Thomas Bewick (7)
Whickham Parochial School

CATS

Cats are great,
Cats are furry things.
They've got four legs
But they don't have wings.

Some eat mice
And rabbits too,
Some eat chunky food,
Ooey-goo!

Some eat codfish
Some eat trout
If you've got a goldfish
You'd better watch out.

Cats are very hairy
They make you sneeze
If you've got asthma
They can make you wheeze

But when you're lonely
And feeling blue
Your cat will always
Be there for you.

Liam Anderson (8)
Whickham Parochial School

BESIDE THE SEA

I love it at the beach collecting shells.
There are so many different smells.

I love to play in the sand.
The way the sand flows through my hand.

Seaweed, crabs, starfish and eels
But how I'd love to see dolphins and seals.

The way the wind blows through my hair
As I watch the birds flying through the air.

The feel of the sun upon my face.
How I love this wonderful and peaceful place.

The waves as they break upon the shore.
I remember other times I've been here before.

My favourite place to be is right here,
Beside the sea.

Brooke Cairns (9)
Whickham Parochial School

WHEN I WALK ALONG THE BEACH

When I walk along the beach I see . . .
Turquoise waves crashing against the sharp ragged rocks.

When I walk along the beach I see . . .
A tall red and white lighthouse blinking in the distance.

When I walk along the beach I see . . .
Hermit crabs hiding in-between the cracks deep in the slimy rock pool.

When I walk along the beach I see . . .
Mermaids making pearl necklaces as they dance under the stars.

When I walk along the beach I see . . .
Multicoloured fish racing to the sandy shore.

When I walk along the beach I see . . .
Golden starfish sunbathing on the rocks with their arms stretched
out wide.

When I walk along the beach I hear . . .
The dolphins singing goodbye as they swim into the distance.

Sophie Dorner (8)
Whickham Parochial School

FOOTBALL FRENZY

In with the plug, on with the switch,
Quick as a flash, they're on the pitch.

The crowd shove, then they roar.
I wonder who will be the first to score?

Shearer is taking a penalty kick,
He boots it into the netting quick!

The crowd scream, they jump up and doon.
Is this going to be another win for the Toon?

The opposition are on the ball,
A shot at goal, what a close call!

A good match for the team,
An end to a perfect dream!

Adam Berkeley (8)
Whickham Parochial School

THE GEEZERS

Julius Caesar was a geezer
who came to old England
he came with ships and infantry
and a great big marching band!

Old Brits were good but not that good
and Caesar knew he was in deep
but soon he turned the tide in style
and the Brits became in a big heap.

He did not hang around too long
because he did not like the scoff
and we had to wait 100 years
until Claudius finished them off.

David Goldsmith (8)
Whickham Parochial School

SEASONS

Autumn is mellow
Leaves brown and yellow

Wintertime of snow and ice
It's not always very nice

Spring birds are singing, flowers are popping up,
Lambs being born, lighter mornings and easier getting up

Summer, holidays camping, beach and sun
Long light nights to play and have fun.

Alex Robinson (8)
Whickham Parochial School

A BORING FLIGHT

We had a boring flight
Which wasn't a delight,
Because we travelled to Africa, it wasn't much fun,
Because all we could see was the rising sun.
We couldn't land in Africa so we landed in Bombay
And that wasn't the way
I planned my day
But I still had a smashing day
                    In Bombay!

Jairaj Lalli (8)
Whickham Parochial School

MY FAMILY

I think my family are nice.
The girls are full of sugar and spice.
The boys, though, aren't quite as good
But Grandma makes a smashing pud.

I have nine cousins in my family.
The youngest one of them is Emily.
Another one of my cousins is called Gemma.
She's always happy, no matter whatever.

In the summer I have lots of fun.
I go to my uncle's and play in the sun.
My family buy me lots of treats,
Sometimes they take me out to eat.

Sometimes my dad can be quite funny,
I love to help spend all his money.
My mam, she works at a school
Which goes to show she's no fool!

They always support me all the way
Watching and helping every day
And I know my family are always there
Whenever I need some help or care.

Laura Convery (8)
Whickham Parochial School

MY NAUGHTY LITTLE SISTER

My naughty little sister *bangs* on my door.
My naughty little sister makes a mess on the floor.
My naughty little sister won't let me be and she always follows me.
My naughty little sister eats like a boar,
That's how most of it gets on the *floor.*
My naughty little sister won't go away when I
Roar!

Joel Nickerson (9)
Whickham Parochial School

THERE'S A NEW MEMBER IN OUR FAMILY

There's a new member in our family
And she's a baby girl.
She's so cute and cuddly
And she's got a golden curl.
She gurgles when she's hungry,
She giggles when she's happy.
She cries when she needs to have a new nappy.
She's really quite nocturnal
And sleeps through the day.
She seems to always get her own way.
Her name is Milly,
No it's not Molly
 And she's not had a ride in a shopping trolley!
Some babies are quite like that
But not this little girl.
This little baby really has changed our world.

Rachel Hirst (8)
Whickham Parochial School

SCHOOLDAYS

I hate school
I'd rather play in the pool
I rule the school
The teacher's just a fool

We have made a Christmas card
We want a roller coaster in the yard
We want the teacher whacked
We all think it's a very good fact

I want a ball all the time
The teacher always drinks lemon and lime
I don't like the teacher
Some   times he's a preacher

I want to play
All day
We always do maths
I'd rather have cosy baths

The teacher's not very good
We never play with wood
We never follow the rules
The teacher calls us fools

I hate wearing ties
I love flies
I hate wearing bobbles
The equipment always wobbles

I hate learning
My brain is always burning
Why can't we keep pets
And fly jets?

Stephanie Gentles (9)
Whickham Parochial School

124

WANTED

There was a dog who had no home
Every day he spent alone
He scampered through bins
For scraps of food
Nobody would feed him
Nobody cared
That's when we met him on the street
We gave relief to his tired feet
We gave him a bed, also some food
His name is 'Wanted' and that's what we've proved
A dog out there needs some help
Give them a chance.

Jordan Gray (8)
Whickham Parochial School

FLICK, FLACK

Practising hard every day and night
for the flick, flack competition.
Trying not to break into a sweat
up and down the tumble track.

Coaches screaming like wailing cats
trying to explain this and that
handstands, cartwheels, forward rolls
trying to make them perfect.

The competition is in two weeks
everyone is very nervous
thinking that they will fall flat
on that dreaded tumble track

Dazzling leotards in the spotlight
glittering hair all up tight
tittle-tattle, lots of spite
coaches giving us some advice.

The music twinkles and the lights fade
as I present to the judges on competition day
now it's my turn to do flick, flacks
up and down, hoping that I'll win that shiny crown

I've done my part and I've done my best
it's up to the judges to decide the rest
and then the moment comes . . . !

Amy Bolam (8)
Whickham Parochial School

MY SWIMMING LESSON

Everyone starts to make a splash,
And the water starts to crash.
Everybody is swimming in the pool,
I think my teacher is quite cruel!
She makes us swim, she makes us dive,
Oh, I do hope I'll survive.
Backstroke, front crawl and even butterfly,
Not some more sculling, I think I will die!
We have to do it from the start
Come on, it's your part.
I think my heart is going to burst,
Now I'm dying of thirst.
I hope I will get something to drink,
But not too much or I'll sink!

Jennifer Spencer (8)
Whickham Parochial School

PENNY

Clouds in the sky and long green grass
Walking by is a very small lass
In her hand on the leader
Something fat and a very messy feeder
It's got small ears, a very wet nose
A little bit of hair and trotters for toes
A tail that's small and curls around
Out if its mouth all you'll hear is a grunting sound
A pot-bellied pig is her pet called Penny
One that caught her eye from a litter of many
She takes her for walks every day into town
Some people stare, laughing, others frown
She takes her for her dinner then home for her bath
Seeing her in water always makes her laugh
Soap on her hair and bubbles on her chin
Splashing around she bares a cheeky grin
As she lifts her out she gets away
She's running wild, Penny wants to play
Penny shakes her body, there is water everywhere
She'll get told off by her mam but Penny doesn't care
The table goes over, on the floor falls the lamp
Penny's on the bed, the sheet's all damp
'Please stop,' shouts the lass but Penny doesn't listen
She hides the lamp but her mam will know it's missing
A key in the front door, footsteps on the stair
She know what will happen, it's simply not fair
A lot of shouts and screams, Penny hides her head
If it wasn't for these lovely people Penny would be dead.
In from school, calling for Penny to come, no response.

'Where's Penny?' she shouts to her mam.
'Penny has gone to a big home far away!'
Tears run down her face, she knows that's where she'll stay
Best friends forever, that's what she will play
Hoping she'll see her Penny some day.

Brooke Black (9)
Whickham Parochial School

TWO LITTLE PUPPIES

Two little puppies
One wintry night
Began to bark
And then to bite

One had a bone
The other had none
And that was why
The barking began

'I want that bone,'
Said the bigger dog
'I had it hidden
Under the log.'

They growled and they barked
That stormy night
It went on for hours
Until it was light

Their owner came
And threw them outside
Without the bone
And nowhere to hide

From all of the wind
The cold and the rain
They huddled together
Friends again!

Steffie Loughlen (10)
Whickham Parochial School

FOOTBALL CRAZY

Football is the game to play
You can play it any day
Pass the ball and score some goals
This is how you play, you know.

Dribbling, tackling, scoring
That's the way we play
Any day, every day!

James Nicholson (9)
Whickham Parochial School

THE GREENKEEPER

I know a greenkeeper called Tony,
his legs are thin and bony,
he drives a tractor around the course
with his bacon bun and brown sauce
he drives around every day
to make sure it's OK
he cuts the grass, he waters the greens
he even checks the grassy denes
he keeps the course looking fine
the halfway hole is number nine.

James Simpson (9)
Whickham Parochial School

CRICKET

Cricket is the game to play,
you can join in any day.
Get your bat, get your ball,
be ready in case you hear the call.
Shane Warne is the best,
he is better than the rest.
When he spins, watch it bounce,
or you could end up getting
trounced!

When you pick up your bat,
don't forget to put on your hat.
If the sun is high in the sky,
make sure you shade your eyes.
If the ball is moving fast,
hit it hard, straight past.
Over the boundary, it's a six!
Let's make sure we have some
great hits!

James Harrison (10)
Whickham Parochial School

MY FISH

In my kitchen live my fish, next to a purple dish,
Max 2 and Elm are their names and they like to play chasey games.
They have shiny scales and see-through tails.
They eat flaky fish food, they think it is quite good.
I'm as happy as can be, because they belong to me.

Martin Walton (9)
Whickham Parochial School

FAIRY-TALE CREATURES

Elves are fair
With long slender hair,
Like lightning they streak
On horses that speak.

Dwarves, underground they dwell
And go to dinner at the sound of a bell,
They make great mines
Which are made in straight lines.

All dragons have claws
And can make tremendous roars,
They have hoards of gold
And have eaten many knights bold

Sorcerers wear pointed hats
And turn people into bats,
They use a staff and whisper a spell
They keep it a secret and never tell.

Trolls are tall and grey as stone
Living off meat and bone,
A hammer he wields
As he smashes shields.

These dark spirits wear a cloak
And their bodies look like smoke,
The dark spirits ride through the night
Spreading fear and spreading fright.

Daniel Hinds (10)
Whickham Parochial School

THE SPIDER

Black and hairy the spider is,
With great big furry legs like twigs.
Its eyes glow red
Under the bed.
What a scary spider this is!

He lives in dark, scary places
And brings fear to many faces.
His web he spins,
Between dustbins.
What a scary spider this is!

His victims could be a bug or a fly,
To escape they really try and try.
But he never fears,
Because he is near.
What a scary spider this is!

Many a time he has dodged a shoe,
It may have even been me or you.
He once was nearly mush
But hid under a bush.
What a *lucky* spider this is!

Craig Hinds (10)
Whickham Parochial School

SPACE

The planets and space,
all one huge race.

The stars and a comet,
fast like Wallace and Gromit!

A very bright sunbeam,
some things aren't the way they seem.

You've read this poem, now I close my case,
the only thing I was on about was that amazing place of,
space!

Patrick Helm (10)
Whickham Parochial School